HOME
&
AWAY
SPECIAL

Written and edited by Clive Hopwood
with contributions by Kate Bryson, Jean Hawkes,
Mike Kidson, Roy Lakeman, Eithne Power,
John Smallwood and Valerie Wooding

Designed by Ian Gwilt

© 1990 World International Publishing Ltd.
All rights reserved.
Published in Great Britain by
World International Publishing Ltd.,
An Egmont Company, Egmont House,
P.O. Box 111, Great Ducie Street,
Manchester M60 3BL.
Printed in Italy. ISBN 0 7235 6899 5

Picture Credits
Australian Tourist Commission pages
2–3,17,18–19,30,36–37,50,52–53,56,62–63
Colorsport pages 31,41,60
The Illustrated London News Picture Library page 23
London Features International Ltd. pages 4,6,9,11,12,16,22,32,38,40,44,58
Scope Features pages 25,26,42,43,51
Syndication International (1986) Ltd. pages 5,7,24,34,35,46,47,48,54
Topham Picture Library pages 13,33,42/43,51,60
World Press Network pages 8,14,20,23,27,28,48

Cover photos supplied by London Features International Ltd. and
Syndication International (1986) Ltd.

*This is an independent publication unconnected with any individual artist,
the television series or the production company. We regret we are unable
to answer personal queries about the programme.*

£4.25

CONTENTS

WALKING ON AIR

They're calling them the Teen Soaps, the top
Aussie soaps that have taken Britain by storm
over the last three years. **Home and Away** and
Neighbours are regularly voted top TV show by
youngsters of all ages, from tiny tots to
teenagers.

Certainly, along with all their fresh air and
sunshine, the Aussie soaps introduced us to a lot
more young characters than have ever been seen
in their British counterparts. Indeed these
young characters immediately went on to
become stars of the soaps, leaving the adults to
provide the solid support.

Home and Away burst onto our screens in
February 1989, as an ITV rival to the BBC's
runaway success *Neighbours*. The setting in
Summer Bay, and the characters of Bobby,
Carly, Steven, Frank and the others went down
very well. Pretty soon there were 14 million of
us (and rising) taking our daily dose of sensation
by the sea and lapping up every minute of it.

Many a household must have slowed to a
complete standstill between 5.30 and 6.30 in
the evening, as fans addicted to the Aussie soaps
sat down to their double helping of the sunshine
sagas. **Home and Away** continues its climb in
popularity, and the addition of new young stars
to replace those departing will doubtless do
much to improve it still further.

Little did we Poms know that exporting
convicts to the far side of the world would result
200 years later in the Aussies exporting soap
operas back to us. And this is only the
beginning . . .

In the Beginning

When it was first screened in Perth **Home and Away** clocked up a massive 37 per cent of the audience against a miserable 3 per cent for rival *Neighbours*. Network Seven's smash hit had proved itself a worthy challenger to Australia's top soap . . . and it was only a matter of time before British TV bosses swooped to pluck another Aussie winner for our screens.

But it wasn't all plain sailing Down Under. The newcomer had initially struggled to establish itself, but fortunately survived long enough to gain a firm place in the top three soaps in Australia, *Neighbours* and *E Street* being the other two.

Set in 'the sun-bleached, surf-lapped town of Summer Bay', **Home and Away** was the idea of producer Alan Bateman. ''I wanted to make an Australian drama that dealt with the hopes,

WELCOME TO

aspirations and fears of young people,'' he explains. ''If you've got twee little children dressed up and saying twee little middle-class things, then it will have no relevance and therefore no relationship to the kids, and they just won't watch.''

The storylines set out to tackle topics relevant to a younger audience. ''The things that concern kids today, and probably always concerned them,'' continues Alan, ''like getting a job, staying at school, drinking and sex, are all covered as part of the theme of **Home and Away**.''

Although it was bought by ITV as a challenger to *Neighbours* they decided that direct competition, through screening at the same time, was likely to be a losing battle. It proved a shrewd move as **Home and Away** climbed steadily to an audience of 14 million over its first twelve months.

If fans gave it the thumbs up, some of the critics were less than kind when it opened. ''The dramatic content and acting are somewhat basic,'' pronounced *Television Today*. ''Right up

to the usual standard,'' said the *Saffron Walden Weekly News*; ''cardboard sets and speech therapy acting, this is a cheap, tatty anachronism; a real throwback to the primal sludge of mass produced, low budget time fillers. It's dull and pedestrian fare.'' (One wonders if 14 million people would want to read the paper!)

The *Yorkshire Post* found that ''it was a slow and discouraging start'' and that it had a ''handful of incompetent child actors.'' Over at the *Northamptonshire Evening Telegraph* their critic found that ''the real disaster is the cast are as wooden as wardrobes and the script just as nauseous as *Neighbours*'', while the *Hampstead and Highgate Express* pointed out that it ''features more fat characters than the anorexic inmates of Ramsay Street. And that is its only point of interest.''

14 million Britons disagree with the critics, as usual, and **Home and Away** proved to be the hit they all obviously hoped it wouldn't be, attracting both the teenage audience it was aimed at, as well as a sizeable following among the over-45s.

The Fletcher Family

The heart of **Home and Away** is the Fletcher Family. Tom and Pippa, unable to have children of their own, decided to raise a foster family instead. Financial problems caused through Tom losing his job brought them to Summer Bay, where they took on the job of managing the local caravan park . . . and calming the locals' fears of delinquents running wild.

The stories and characters are based on real life case histories, featuring children whose parents were criminals, alcoholics, child batterers or dead. They provided endless possibilities for stories dealing head-on with social problems.

TOM FLETCHER (*Roger Oakley*) was a foster child himself. A Vietnam War veteran, he is a dreamer and an idealist. His decision to foster clearly

CARLY MORRIS (*Sharyn Hodgson*) is a bright and vivacious teenager. Although she adored her mother, relations with her father were very strained. Argument and confrontation were the result, and her father ended up beating her. When her mother died, another beating from her father led to her being taken into care, and later fostered by Tom and Pippa.

STEVEN MATHESON (*Adam Willits*) saw his parents killed when their house burned down. A clever, but deeply disturbed young man, he was initially prone to terrible nightmares about his parents' death. Tom and Pippa helped to fill the awful vacuum left by the loss of the mum and dad he loved so much.

SALLY KEATING (*Kate Richie*) is the youngest of the foster children. Her parents drowned when she was three, and Sally went to live with her

SUMMER BAY

stems from his own childhood; his mother had fostered him out at the age of two after his father had deserted them both at birth. A caring and understanding dad, Tom tries to give each of his foster children the love and attention he himself missed as a child.

PIPPA FLETCHER (*Vanessa Downing*) has been married to Tom for 12 years, and readily agreed to Tom's idea about fostering. She gave up her job to become a full-time mum. She believes in the gentle touch and tries to treat the children in her care with kindness and affection, rather than as a stern authority figure. Good-hearted and honest, Pippa is nevertheless not afraid to speak her mind.

FRANK MORGAN (*Alex Papps*) was the first of the foster children. He comes from the background of a criminal father and an alcoholic mother. Streetwise Frank fell foul of the law himself at the tender age of eight. It was at this point that Frank was fostered, and ultimately Tom and Pippa became the parents he always wanted.

grandmother. When her granny developed Alzheimer's disease Sally was put into a home,

where – out of loneliness – she invented an imaginary friend, Milko. She moved in with the Fletchers with her friend LYNN DAVENPORT, who she met in the home.

BOBBY SIMPSON (*Nicolle Dickson*) already had a reputation for being a rebel and a delinquent in Summer Bay before the Fletchers arrived. A very aggressive character with few friends, she was expelled from the local school by deputy headmaster, DONALD FISHER (*Norman Coburn*), who she later discovered to be her real father. Initially helped by AILSA STEWART (*Judy Nunn*), Bobby finds the family she longed for in the friendly Fletchers.

BRIAN SIMPSON (*Terry Donovan*) is Bobby's missing 'father' who turns up in Summer Bay and crosses swords with Fisher, about whom he knows some dark and murky secret.

RUTH STEWART (*Justine Clark*), better known as Roo, is the only child of ALF STEWART (*Ralph Meagher*). Her mother died from drowning, and she found it particularly difficult to come to terms with a new mum. When Alf fell in love with the keeper of the local grocery store, Ailsa Hogan, Roo rebelled, but Ailsa's warm, generous nature eventually won her over. Ailsa, however, has something of a mysterious past.

CELIA STEWART (*Fiona Spence*) and MORAG BELLINGHAM (*Cornelia Francis*) are two sides of a coin. Celia, quiet and conservative, contrasts with her more ruthless and scheming sister, Morag.

WELCOME TO SUMMER BAY

MARILYN CHAMBERS (*Emily Symons*) is pretty and bubbly, with a generous dash of zaniness, and a tendency to be accident prone. Target of her energetic affections is the hapless Lance.

GRANT MITCHELL (*Craig McLachlan*) is a hunky teacher at the local school with unorthodox teaching methods, and one or two skeletons rattling quietly in the cupboard.

BEN LUCINI (*Julian McMahon*) is a soldier of Italian extraction who ditches the army when he falls for Carly and Summer Bay.

LANCE (*Peter Vroom*) and MARTIN (*Craig Thomson*) provide the comic relief in Summer Bay, and are always coming up with madcap – and usually totally disastrous – schemes.

MATT (*Greg Benson*) is the local lifeguard and ace surfer, whose looks are enough to make any female volunteer to be rescued and given the kiss of life, preferably several times.

HOME + AWAY

With his dark sensual looks and his devastating smile, romantic newcomer Alex Papps has sent pulses racing on both sides of the globe since his arrival as **Home and Away**'s Frank Morgan. But fame has also brought its rising young star his share of problems.

RELUCTANT IDOL

Alex Papps

Frank

"I got into acting because I like acting," says Alex, "but there are days when you question your reasons for being in it." Coping with the adulation can be very difficult, since Alex denies that he's a heart-throb. "It's not that I disapprove of the word, it's just that it's not me," he says modestly.

Alex is essentially a very private person, and he admits to being a home bird. "My home is my castle," says Alex. "Nothing is more relaxing than watching a bit of telly, playing some music on the piano and just being able to relax in my room with all my stuff around me, my pictures, photographs, and posters."

The tumultuous romantic career of Frank in **Home and Away** bears little resemblance to Alex's own life. He has had no girlfriend since his relationship with actress Nadine Gardner split up last year. Right now Alex has other priorities. "A relationship for me at the moment would be difficult. It's easier to be alone. When you're in a good relationship it's great. But I'm finding that my independence is far more important, so a girlfriend is out."

But his family continues to give valuable support, and he sees them as much as he can. Both his parents are theatre directors, but even coming from a showbiz background was little preparation for the scale of adoration that Alex meets.

"I'm not in this for the fame and publicity," says Alex. "If girls scream I figure they are screaming for Frank, not me. I read articles about myself and I have no idea whatsoever who the person is they are writing about."

Even teenage boys envy him. They would love to be the object of such female adulation and receive sackfuls of devoted fan mail. But Alex says he finds it all rather a drag. "I'd much rather be a rock and roller than a soap star," he reveals. "I get all this mail from girls who scream at me, but I'm not going to let it go to my head. In fact I do my best to stay away from crowds."

Alex is quite determined that success is not going to change him. "It's so easy for people in my profession to use their fame to bolster their egos," says Alex. "I try not to let it influence my way of thinking."

Home and Away wasn't Alex's first experience of Australian TV. He has appeared in *The Henderson Kids* (opposite Nadine Gardner), *Prisoner: Cell Block H* and even *Neighbours*. But fame with a capital F didn't really strike until he landed the lead role in **Home and Away**.

"The media has already stereotyped me," complains Alex. "They can't say Alex Papps is a normal guy because the public just doesn't seem to want to read that sort of thing."

Despite the outside pressures, however, there is a great sense of affection and comradeship among the cast and crew of **Home and Away**. Getting his big break meant moving away from the family home in Melbourne. Living in Sydney, where the soap is shot, made him feel very homesick. To lift his spirits the crew arranged a special birthday surprise for him.

Hidden inside Alex's wardrobe was his teenage sister, Selena, whom the crew had flown in especially. Alex had the shock of his life. "There she was, tied up in a big bow," he laughs.

"I'm not in this for fame and publicity"

Stardom hasn't prevented this serious young man from keeping his feet firmly on the ground. Being away from his family has meant that he has had to learn to rely on himself, and develop strong, personal discipline. Away from TV cameras Alex tries to lead a fairly normal, balanced lifestyle.

He is, amongst other things, a committed environmentalist. "The planet is decomposing," he explains. "We do many things unwittingly to destroy the environment. If you really like something you usually take care of it." Alex recycles all his rubbish, and shops carefully for environmentally friendly goods. He has also joined the Friends of Sherbrooke Forest, a conservation group in Victoria, and the World Wide Fund for Nature.

Alex is perceptive enough to realize that, with no formal acting training, he has a long way to go to prove himself. "I feel very lucky," he says, adding, "but I think it's very dangerous to take it all for granted because it could all go. At least I've made a good start – I'm lucky to

"The media has already stereotyped me"

have this exposure when most actors are struggling."

But acting is what continues to be what gives him most satisfaction. "The greatest thing is that I'm actually doing something that started off as a hobby – and I'm making a living out of it!" As for fame, Alex says, "It's all become too much. I hate it when people call me an idol."

LAURELS FOR POP STAR CRAIG

Martin may be a life-long contender for Nerd of the Year (and who could blame him with a family like his), but actor Craig Thomson enjoys the comedy acting his character requires.

"He's got a heart of gold," says Craig, "but his brain lets him down. Lance and Martin are the Laurel and Hardy of Summer Bay." Mind you, Craig finds the **Home and Away** schedule very tiring, and says he has no plans to join another soap when he eventually leaves.

Craig started acting at school, and went on to study acting full-time at 15. He then moved into commercials before landing the part of Martin. His recent bid for pop stardom looks like proving a success, with a debut album due out this year. Well, Laurel and Hardy had a hit in the top ten not that long ago, so why not?

GREEN GRANT

Grant Mitchell, the teacher played by Craig McLachlan, must be amongst the most environmentally friendly soap characters on our screens. A far cry from cheeky Henry Ramsay, Grant is very keen on green issues.

Explains Craig, "He's into meditation and protecting the ozone layer. He's into protecting just about everything as a matter of fact, from dolphins to stopping wood chipping, you name it." He's also a vegetarian.

Grant comes from a middle-class background. His parents run a business making plastic garden furniture, but Grant turned his back on that to become a teacher. His brother, who is 16, is the budding capitalist in the family, while his 14-year-old sister is into boys, rock music and clothes. Neither appear in the show.

Grant is dedicated to his profession, and has a special rapport with the kids. His teaching methods are occasionally unorthodox, however, and this tends to get him in trouble with his superiors.

WERE HERE

LIFESAVER GREG

The part of lifeguard Matt comes naturally to sea-loving Greg Benson. Having lived by the sea all his life – something his dad ensured – Greg tries to get in a spot of surfing at every available moment, even taking his surf board into work with him. Palm Beach, used for location work, is close to where **Home and Away** is shot, so Greg has chance to ride a few waves in between takes.

Greg's father was very keen on surf lifesaving, and certainly did his best to instil the same enthusiasm into his children. Greg belonged to a lifesaving club from an early age, and the whole family spent lots of time at the beach.

Along with his brother Craig, and sister Tracey, Greg would spend hours messing about in the water with their mates. Dad would regularly whisk the kids away in the family station wagon to learn swimming, fishing and later scuba diving.

So it's no surprise that Greg took to the role of Matt like a duck, or rather a lifeguard, to water.

FUNKY STUFF

Dannii Minogue quit **Home and Away** last June, after her seven-month stint as Emma Jackson. The decision to leave was all part of Dannii's plans to launch herself into the pop world.

At a cost of $50,000 the video of Love and Kisses was made to promote Dannii's first single. Recording and filming was done in New York, with black producers aiming to give her an authentically funky feel to her music.

"A lot of people thought I'd copy Kylie and have a Stock, Aitken and Waterman song and have a sound exactly like hers," says Dannii, "but that's just not the sort of stuff I'd do."

At the time Dannii said, "I have to be confident and aim for a number one. I'm very nervous about how it's going to go and whether people will like it. I just hope it sells enough so I can continue." She should be so lucky, as big sister might have said!

The girl who was voted Britain's best-loved soap star can't understand why. "I haven't got any sex appeal," says 21-year-old Nicolle Dickson. "It's weird." The **Home and Away** star beat 400 other aspiring actresses for the role of delinquent Bobby, and has proved a resounding hit, especially with British viewers.

AN ORDINARY SUBURBAN GIRL

Nicolle Dickson

Bobby

Trucker's daughter Nicolle was working in a factory not too long ago, and nearly didn't make it to stardom at all. Six weeks before Nicolle took her screen test for **Home and Away** she and her sister were involved in a terrifying car crash.

Nicolle admits that a combination of hard work and late nights had made her feel very tired. "I just fell asleep while I was driving," she recalls. "I veered off the road into a telegraph pole. It was awful. My sister's cheekbone was fractured, and I broke my jaw." Nicolle was fined for her driving.

"My jaw was wired up for a month," says Nicolle. "I couldn't eat and had to take liquids through a straw. The wires came off just two weeks before the screen test!" Nicolle went on to win the role, and since then has concentrated on her acting career, even at the expense of romance.

"I had a very special guy," reveals Nicolle, "and we were together for six months. But it had all got too much for me and we split because I couldn't concentrate on my work. It made me realize how important my career is to me."

The pint size soap star, all 4 feet 11 inches of her, kept millions of viewers captivated with her romantic adventures in **Home and Away**. Her search for her real parents kept us all guessing, knowing that someone in Summer Bay was her father. Nicolle didn't altogether

find it easy and work was often not there. "Now people seem to think I have it easy," she laughs. "They don't realize we work a solid five day week!"

Nicolle takes her job seriously and works hard. "I worry about my work on the show," she says. "Sometimes you get stale and dissatisfied. I've gone through stages where I feel I haven't put enough into it. You lose concentration and energy sometimes. You churn it out day after day, and unless you've got a storyline you can lose it."

"I think Bobby's selfish and foolish"

approve. "I think Bobby's selfish and foolish," she feels. "I know a lot of kids who have tried to search for their real parents and it's unfair on the people who brought you up." But Bobby's walk down the aisle with Frank did meet with the independent Nicolle's approval, however, along with millions of viewers.

The fans can sometimes scare Nicolle. "People can be so obsessive. It's terrifying to think they can be so overwhelmed by you. It really puts me on edge when they scream and go crazy. Sometimes I feel like I'm about to break down – it's hard to explain." Not that Nicolle is easily scared. "I've got spunk," she says. "I have never been rebellious although sometimes I can

Whatever her fears she looks back on the last decade as one of great change and amazing good fortune. "It's pretty amazing considering I never really expected to ever get work as an actress!" she exclaims. "I've been very fortunate but titles such as *Most Popular Soap Actress* make me feel nervous. I have to make sure I keep working hard at acting. I don't want this title to be the beginning of the end for me."

Yet another proud achievement came early in 1989 when she won the *Most Popular New Talent in Australia*. "The cast expected I would win this award which made me even more nervous," recalls Nicolle. Minutes after receiving the statuette and a kiss from screen husband, Alex Papps, Nicolle tried ringing her parents with the good news. "But they had changed their telephone number . . . and I couldn't remember it!"

Her family is very important to Nicolle. After a spell living in a fashionable flat in

"I've been very fortunate"

become aggressive. But I'm certainly not a tomboy."

Her own background is that of a very ordinary, suburban girl, she says. One of three daughters of Sydney transport company chief Lester Dickson and his wife Cheryl, Nicolle has always sung and danced since she was a toddler. Determined to become an actress, she didn't

Paddington, Sydney, she moved back to live with her parents. She now lives in a garage – a converted one – adjoining her parents' house, which was originally planned for her grandfather.

And it's her family who have helped withstand the sudden and momentous pressures that come with soap stardom. "Without them I think I would have given up acting," she says. "I

know how I was going to handle the limelight. Now I manage because I know it's part of the

don't think I could have coped." In the meantime Nicolle is learning all the time.

"When I first started in the soap I didn't

job to sell the show and keep people entertained." Inevitably the pressure does get to the young actress. Then, she says, she does the only sensible thing. "I go to my parents and cry."

THE WORLD OF OZ

Australia invented the ballot box in Victoria in 1856. South Australia was the first Australian state to grant the vote to both men (1856) and women (1894).

Western Australia is the largest state, comprising almost a third of the whole country.

Hobart in Tasmania introduced the first parking meters into Australia . . . on April Fool's Day in 1955.

Most of the world's marsupials, over 150 species, live in Australia.

There is no known antidote to a bite from the deadly funnel-web spider. Australia also has the world's most venomous snake – the taipan, found in northern Queensland. Measuring about 10 feet in length, a single taipan carries enough venom to kill 23,000 mice!

Dorothy Williams set a world underground endurance record in 1963 by staying in a cave at Yallugup, Western Australia for 90 days.

The first royal visit to Australia was in 1867, when Alfred, the Duke of Edinburgh, then 23, made a state visit. Someone tried to assassinate him in Sydney.

Australia is 25 times the size of Britain and Ireland.

The first man to cross from Adelaide to the west coast of Australia was E.J. Eyre in 1841. Burke, Wills, King and Gray attempted the crossing from south to north in 1861. Only King survived to tell of their journey.

Melbourne was the first place in Australia to build its own town hall in 1954.

The longest place names in Australia are both lakes – Lake CADIBARRAWIRRACANNA and Lake MIRRANPONGAPONGUNNA.

In 1870 Sidney Kidman, at the age of 13, had five shillings and a one-eyed horse. He went on to own around 100,000 square miles in Central Australia, Queensland and New South Wales, and to win himself a knighthood.

The first postal service in Australia was in Sydney in 1809.

The Flying Pieman, William Francis King, once walked 1,634 miles in 39 days. He also walked from Sydney to Parramatta (15 miles) and back, twice a day for 6 days. Perhaps his most unusual feat was his walk from Campbeltown to Sydney (33 miles) in 8 hours 20 minutes, carrying a 70lb dog!

Between 1788 and 1868 157,000 convicts were transported from Britain to Australia.

Photo by courtesy of the Australian Tourist Commission

A farm in Western Australia

SYDNEY: URBAN CENTRE OF

Seven out of ten Australians live in one of the major cities. All but Canberra, the capital city, are situated on the coast. Australia has the fewest people per square mile than any other country on Earth, and yet more of those people live in cities than anywhere else.

Sydney, Melbourne, Adelaide, Perth, Darwin, Hobart, Canberra. This is what most Australians experience as everyday life – not that much different from people living in other big cities like, London, New York or Paris.

Incredible though it is to inhabitants of a small country like Britain, the distance between some cities in Australia is colossal: Darwin to Melbourne is 2500 miles, Sydney·to Perth the same.

The Opera House

Photos by courtesy of the Australian Tourist Commission

AUSTRALIA

CITY OF GOLDEN SANDS

Sydney, built around one of the most beautiful harbours in the world, boasts more than thirty beaches of golden sands. A city of 3.5 million, the bridge and the magnificent Opera House are its most famous landmarks.

One in four Australians live in Sydney. To some people it *is* Australia. It was, after all, the birthplace of modern Australia. A cosmopolitan city with Anglo-Celtic, Southern and Northern European roots mixed with Southeast Asians and people from the Pacific Islands, Sydney is truly an international centre.

It has plenty to offer. From the surfing beaches like Bondi, to the stunning architecture and high culture of the Opera House; from

The suburb of Paddington

Sydney from the air

Captain/Governor Bligh's House to one of the best live rock circuits in the country; from the wildlife of Taronga Park on Mosman Bay to day trips to Old Sydney Town at Gosford where life as a convict is recreated.

With average summer temperatures of 21.4°C (72.1°F) and 12.6°C (54.1°F) in winter, Sydney does also experience its share of cold, wet and horrible days, and sweltering heat waves. But it never snows in Sydney, and the only ice you'll see will come from the fridge.

For a girl who has usually been overshadowed by her big sister, Dannii Minogue is not doing too badly. But the two sisters are friendly rivals, with no envy or bitterness between them, and delighted that the Minogues are both in vogue.

LITTLE SISTER

Dannii Minogue

Emma

Both sisters had early successes on TV, but it was *Neighbours* that proved the biggest test. Kylie won the role and Dannii lost out. "Mum was really good to me at the time," says Dannii. "She explained that I was only 16 and Kylie was older and had more experience, and that I should learn from that and enjoy the fact that she got the part."

Now Dannii has made her own

international reputation thanks to **Home and Away**. To give authenticity to the part she cut off her curls and turned punk to become Emma Jackson, an incest victim who comes to Summer Bay and the protective foster family of Tom and Pippa Fletcher. "Emma's had a rotten life," says Dannii, "and rebels against her parents – not a bit like me really!"

But being a Minogue has not always been

easy. Explains Dannii, whose real name is Danielle, "A lot of people may try and use me, but I talked all this over with my parents and we picked a good manager who looks after Kylie too." Leaving her family in Melbourne to work on **Home and Away** in Sydney has been a wrench, for Dannii, her parents and the rest of the family are very close.

"Kylie and I are very lucky and can thank our parents for that because they never pushed, just encouraged us," says Dannii. "They helped keep our feet on the ground. We have an extraordinary bond at home because Mum treats us as if we are normal. There is no star treatment. It may sound corny but we're just the kids to her. It's such a relief. When you've got people hunting you for autographs and stopping you in the street, you need a retreat."

"I don't have time for boyfriends"

Time is something busy Dannii is short of these days, however. "The family don't see as much of Kylie and me as they used to, but my mum and dad are very proud of us. I don't have time for boyfriends either. I had been going out with one guy for two years but we've split up. It's hard to combine all I'm doing with a relationship although having someone around like that can give a lot of support."

One thing she does differ from her family on is meat. "I turned vegetarian some time back," explains Dannii, "because I didn't like the taste of meat. Then I did some research and decided it was wrong to eat it. My family weren't too happy to begin with, but now I cook my own meals, so it's okay. And I feel a lot better for it."

Indeed Dannii is feeling very good all round. Having released her first single, the heavy funk number *Love and Kisses*, and her debut album, Dannii has left **Home and Away** and looks like she's trying to catch big sister up by a short cut. So far so good, and Dannii has no regrets.

"Sometimes people tell me I'm missing out on what normal teenagers do," she says. "But in a way I think they're missing out. Sure, the Great Aussie Soap Bubble may burst. But if you're good enough you come through that. I hope I could carry on." Feel free, Dannii – see you in the headlines.

"Emma's had a rotten life"

HOME + AWAY

"The fans think I'm cute," says young Kate Ritchie. "It's very nice, but I'm not a star. I've just been lucky, that's all." Kate's modesty masks an unusually professional approach for one so young, but despite her TV fame she doesn't see her future as an actress.

SUCH FUN

Kate Ritchie

Kate is the daughter of a Sydney policeman, Steve, and his wife, Heather. She is the eldest of four children; Susan is four, Stuart seven, and Rebekah eight. It may come as a surprise to viewers but sister Rebekah also features in **Home and Away** . . . invisibly!

When poor little orphan Sally Keating speaks to her imaginary friend, young actress Kate Ritchie is really speaking to her own sister. 11-year-old Kate thinks of her sister, Rebekah when she has to say those lines. "It's hard to act to thin air," says Kate, "so thinking that I'm talking to Rebekah helps me."

Kate has plenty of people around her to keep her feet on the ground. "I got teased a bit when I started," says Kate, "but now the kids at school treat me as just another ordinary kid. The family aren't the least bit impressed because I'm on television. My parents don't treat me any differently either. I'm still told to go to my room if I'm naughty."

Normal though that may be, Kate's workload is hard going for a young star. "Sometimes we have to get up at five," says her mum, "but she never grumbles. She just gets on with it. She's very professional. Fortunately Kate is very bright at school. It's just as well. We have always said that if ever her studies suffered because of her television work we would have to take her away from TV."

Kate started working in commercials at five, had her own agent at six. She's also tried her hand at writing, producing her own play, *The Magic Rose*, at school. "I don't really want to be an actress when I grow up," reveals Kate,

Sally

"It's hard to act to thin air"

however. "It's all such fun now, but I think I'd rather be a landscape gardener or perhaps an author."

22

AUSTRALIAN GOLD

DAME NELLIE MELBA

She was "The voice of Australia". Born Helen Mitchell on 19th May 1861, she was to grow up in Melbourne, which as a city was barely a quarter of a century old.

A real prima donna, a natural opera singer, she could be generous – and mean, kindly but also ruthless. As Nellie Melba she was to tour the great opera houses of the world.

Despite early opposition from her parents, she made her first professional appearance in Melbourne in 1884, her international debut in Brussels in 1887. It was said of her that "she is the Queen of Song in an era of Great Singers". It was in December 1887 that she adopted the name Melba, after her beloved home city.

In the whole history of opera there is said to have been no more exceptional figure. She did not, as expected, spend hours practising, she merely ran up and down a few scales daily, to keep her voice 'oiled' as she called it. But when she sang with the Great Caruso at Monte Carlo the audience were in awe.

She was honoured as a Dame in 1918. During the Great War she had raised $500,000 for the Red Cross. She died quite suddenly in 1931, while on a trip back to Australia, and is buried in Melbourne.

Peach Melba and Melba Toast are both named after her.

DAWN FRASER

Born on 4th September 1937, Dawn Fraser truly became "The Queen of Swimming". She was the only pool competitor to win the same Olympic title three times. She won the gold medal for the 100m freestyle in 1956, 1960 and 1964.

In the first of these victories she beat her team mate, Lorraine Crapp, by 0.3 seconds, setting a new world record of 62.0 seconds. In 1960 and 1964 she broke her own records, with 61.2 in Rome and 59.5 in Tokyo. This made her the first woman to break the minute barrier for the 100m freestyle.

Originally from Adelaide, her swimming took her all over the world. In her ten year career she won eight Commonwealth medals, six of them gold. Altogether she won 23 Australian titles - the 100m freestyle (7 times), the 200m freestyle (8 times), the butterfly 100m (twice) and the individual medley 200m (once). She held 27 individual world records.

In 1964 this extraordinary woman was voted Australian of the Year as a mark of respect for her work. But her relationship with authority was not all that it might have been. She was fiery and very independent. Her career sadly ended when, after the 1964 Olympics, she was suspended for 10 years for misbehaviour.

The sporting world was shocked that such a bright star should fall so far so fast, but few have blazed so brilliantly.

THE SOAPIES

Australian soap opera's rise to the top

We all know about Australian soaps – in fact, most of us watch them! But did you know that the first 'homegrown' Australian soap, or soapie, was made less than twenty years ago? In that time the soapies have become far more than simply cheap, daytime fillers and have gone on to conquer huge audiences on the other side of the world, particularly in Britain.

Number 96 started it all. Until the 1970s Australian TV relied very heavily on imported programmes, notably from the USA. In 1973 Australia's commercial Channel 10 was struggling with falling ratings, and executive Ian Holmes decided that a good, original soap might save the day. He devised the idea of a daily drama involving characters living in a block of flats, and passed it on to two producers with the suggestion that the script be kept spicy. The result was skilfully promoted – as "the night television lost its virginity" – and *Number 96* was soon topping the ratings.

As a soap it was original in two respects. Firstly, it was broadcast at prime time, five nights a week - a new departure for Australian television. Secondly, it dealt with adult themes. Perhaps for that reason it was never broadcast in Britain.

FAMILY AT WAR

Although *Number 96* demonstrated to Australian broadcasters and viewers how effective soaps could be, it was by no means the only influence on their subject matter. One of the oldest soapies, and the first to be shown in Britain, was *The Sullivans*. Developed in response to the popularity in Australia of Granada TV's *A Family At War*, it followed the fortunes of the Sullivan family, their friends and neighbours, during the years of the Second World War and immediately afterwards.

A carefully researched and thoughtful series, *The Sullivans* has proved much more popular with viewers around the world than the more sensational soaps. It has been shown in more than thirty countries, and more than once in Britain.

DOCTORS

Just as old as *The Sullivans* is a serial
with a classic soap theme, one which
found a responsive audience in Britain.
Medical soaps have long been popular
here, and *The Young Doctors* proved to
be no exception. It relates the
adventures – romantic, comic and
otherwise – of the staff of the Albert
Memorial Hospital.

Seen nowadays it looks rather dated,
offering plenty of scope for spotters of
1970s fashions! Spotters of future soap
stars are also accommodated by it:
during its five-year run *The Young
Doctors* provided many of the famous
faces of more recent soaps with valuable
experience.

PRISONERS

One of the natural successors to
Number 96, in its more adult tone if not
in its content, has gone on to become a
hit with British late-night audiences.
Prisoner: Cell Block H, devised in 1979
by Grundy Television's Reg Watson, is
set in the fictional Wentworth Detention
Centre. The stories centre round a tough
group of women prisoners and warders.
Described by critics as "a hellhouse of
appalling animalistic behaviour", it deals
with its grim premise and its cast of
murderers, robbers and sadistic warders
with brutal, if melodramatic, frankness.

It's a far cry from the gentler worlds of
family life which are the principal subject
matter of the latterday **Home and Away**
and *Neighbours*! It remains an
interesting reminder that soaps can
come in all shades, and *Prisoner: Cell
Block H* is one of the more interesting
experiments into the darker side of soap.

Although *Prisoner* ended its Australian run in 1986, it remains a firm favourite in Britain, and has even spawned a successful touring stage version in this country.

FAMILY FEUD

Another soap that has enjoyed popularity in Britain is the melodramatic *Sons and Daughters*. Based on the traditional theme of conflict and misunderstanding between two feuding families, this soap enjoyed a long run in Australia, lasting from 1981 to 1987.

One key breakthrough *Sons and Daughters* did achieve was to manage to bridge the soap gap between rivals Sydney and Melbourne, placing one family in each. Audiences particularly enjoyed the bitchy character of Pat 'the rat' Hamilton, played with great relish by English-born Rowena Wallace.

LOCAL VET

Medical matters received a slightly different treatment when *A Country Practice* began running. This heart-warming series has gone on to become one of Australia's most popular soaps, and has won devoted fans here in Britain too. The story of isolated Wandin Valley and its residents, centres around the local vet's, and has a reputation for its social messages, mixed in with a fair helping of romance.

It has a wholesome, small town charm about it, rather like that of *The Waltons*. First made in 1981 *A Country Practice* is still in production, and a firm favourite with Australian audiences.

FIRST WAVE

These six soaps give you some idea of the scope of the first wave from Australia. Although popular in Britain

they have never attracted audiences large enough to compete on equal terms with our own *Coronation Street* and *EastEnders*.

The crucial breakthrough, so far as viewing figures counted, was to come with the second wave of soapies, which particularly appealed to younger audiences. It was only a footstep away . . .

NEIGHBOURS

The success story of the saga of Ramsay Street is well known. Brought to the screen in 1985 by Ian Holmes and Reg Watson, *Neighbours* survived being cancelled in its early days. A greater emphasis on the street's younger residents was a noticeable factor in its later success as the first of the Aussie 'teen soaps'.

In Britain, the decision to move the soap to a 5.30pm slot immediately doubled its viewing figures, and it became the first Australian programme ever to challenge Britain's established favourites head on. Curiously no one, including the actors on the show, has been fully able to account for its extraordinary success over here.

HOME AND AWAY

The launch of **Home and Away** in 1988 was soon to build on its predecessor's popularity, and has climbed steadily in the ratings. Its young stars have won it an impressive following. A survey conducted in early 1990 by girls' comic, *Bunty*, indicated that readers thought it the better of the two teen soaps.

Which will come out on top eventually is open to question, although in Australia *Neighbours* is still ahead in the ratings. They are, however, not alone . . . here's a quick look at what is currently on offer in Australia, in addition to *Neighbours, A Country Practice*, and **Home and Away**.

WATERING HOLES

Launched in early 1990 by Channel 9, *Family and Friends* is concerned with the lives and loves of two feuding families (sound a familiar theme?), the Rossis and the Chandlers, over three generations. Developed by Alan Bateman, the man behind **Home and Away**, it combines the nostalgic appeal of *The Sullivans* (also a Channel 9 show) with the emphasis on present-day romances, and plenty of over-the-top melodrama. In episode one the lovers met, discussed the full moon, fell in love, fell out with their families, and then fell down a well. Nothing like starting off the way you mean to go on, although early viewer reaction was not very encouraging.

Then there is *E Street*, already well established, whose stories revolve around the lives of the people in Patchett's Bar, with some of the adult content of *Number 96*. Supported by supersoaps *The Flying Doctors and GP* (they're clearly keen on doctors Down Under!), the soapies are in good form.

FAMILIES

This is one Aussie soap we could be sure of seeing on our screens over here. Granada TV invested £3 million in the making of *Families*, filming in both Sydney on location and in the studio in Manchester, with a mixed English and Australian cast. As the ratings war hots up this could represent the beginning of a third wave . . . of home-grown British soapies.

You've got to hand it to Craig McLachlan for sheer nerve, leaping straight from one top Australian soap to another – its deadliest rival. **Home and Away** gained while *Neighbours* lost, but it all kept Craig's fans mighty happy to know he'd still be on our screens.

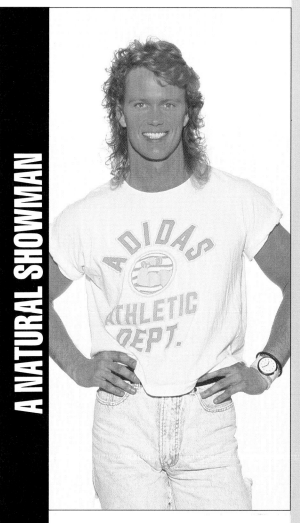

A NATURAL SHOWMAN

Channel 7, to join their successful teen soap, **Home and Away**. The goodies on offer were reported to include £1 million and promises of a lead Hollywood role.

Said Craig, "They fought hard to get me, and one of the reasons I accepted was the chance to do movies. The network has links with NBC in the States, so I've been screen testing for an American mini-series."

"I'm a fitness fanatic"

Craig made his first appearance in Australia in **Home and Away** last February. He joined the cast as inspirational young teacher, Grant Mitchell, who works at Summer Bay College. (Grant is, of course, no relation to the Mitchells from *Neighbours*!)

All the female students want to be teacher's pet, including one by the name of Karen – played, coincidentally, by Danielle (Dannii) Minogue, whose sister you may have heard of.

Says Craig, "Grant doesn't have a lot of boisterousness in him, but he is likeable all the same. He's into meditation and conservation

Craig McLachlan   Grant

Only three years ago Craig was an unknown making his debut on *Neighbours*, and definitely a member of the supporting cast. But in that time he has developed the character of ex-jailbird Henry into a starring role, and moved up into soap stardom and recording contracts.

Craig was never one to do things the conventional way, and at the peak of his stardom he accepted an offer from rival network,

and the students really dig him. Without giving too much away, there are a few surprises in store when 'Cool Mitch', as he is dubbed, prepares for a weightlifting contest. He comes to be regarded as rather unorthodox in his teaching methods . . . but that depends on your viewpoint."

The script calls for Craig to bare that manly chest as often as possible. Fortunately it's a well-developed chest, and reckoned to be well worth baring. "I'm a fitness fanatic," reveals Craig. "I have been for years. I work out for up to two hours a day, four days a week. Weight training is like a live-in psychiatrist for me. Pumping iron gets rid of all my frustrations. It stops me giving people the elbow. It keeps me sane."

Craig's new management are not terribly keen on his musclebound, hunky image. They want their man to become more mature – a sort of shining, smiling, singing, international megastar with toothpaste teeth, bags of future and no past.

A hard task if you look at his life so far. "I was a disappointment to my parents in my schooldays," admits Craig. "I wasn't an academic like the rest of the family and relations. All my school reports said things like, 'Craig has ability if only he would settle down and stop trying to make people laugh all the time.' Some hope! If I could make the class laugh I felt real good, and if I could make the teacher laugh that was a bonus."

He was ever the showman, a natural performer. "I was always singing into Mum's

"It's a delicate juggling routine at the moment," says Craig. "I don't know how long I can walk on the tightrope between the two. I'm still managing to keep abreast of it, and maintain some sanity, although people would argue the sanity part!"

"Give me a stage! I want to perform!"

vacuum cleaner hose, for example," laughs Craig. "For years my family were convinced there was something wrong with my brainpower. They were well-educated and successful in business, while I kept saying, 'Give me a stage! I want to perform!'"

After a couple of uncertain starts Craig's first break came with a role in the soap *The Young Doctors*. This led to another part in *Sons and Daughters*, and this in its turn got him an audition for *Neighbours*. All this time Craig had been loyally supported by his wife, Karen, who acted as his manager. This arrangement continued until Craig and Karen sadly parted, Craig blaming the pressures of his work as the cause of the breakdown.

Craig is a self-confessed workaholic. As well as working on soaps and other TV projects, he·is also pursuing a music career with a nine album deal already signed with CBS Records.

With so much to fill his time it's hard to imagine any woman seriously expecting to keep hold of Craig for long. Besides there is something in him that is permanently seeking to draw attention to himself. Anne Barnes, who has known him since he was a little boy, recalls making a home video of him, celebrating winning the role in *Neighbours*. "He was so excited, as soon as I got the camera out he went mad. He was always an exhibitionist, and in seconds he was dancing around and taking his trousers off. He always loved dropping his pants for a joke, but his wife Karen was not amused."

It's not exactly the behaviour that his management would imagine being appropriate to an international megastar either, now is it? Even now one can see them scribbling a note in the book: 'Craig has ability if only he would settle down and stop trying to make people laugh all the time.' But that, after all, is simply Craig being himself and we wouldn't want him any other way.

THE WORLD OF OZ

More people are killed by sharks off the Australian east coast than anywhere else in the world. The most popular times for attacks are between 3pm and 6pm in January . . . in four feet of water, between 10–50 yards off shore.

Granny Smith apples come from Australia. They were first cultivated by Maria Ann Smith at Eastwood in New South Wales in the 1860s.

The first shots fired in the British Empire after the declaration of war in 1914 were in Melbourne. Fort Nepean opened fire on the German freighter *Pfalz*. Australia was also the only dominion to form its own air force during World War I.

World champion sheep shearer Kevin Sarre of Victoria sheared 327 merinos in 7 hours 40 minutes in a record-breaking effort in 1957.

In 1930 a tweed suit was made in 1 hour 50 minutes – from the moment the wool left the sheep's back to the moment it went on a man as a finished suit.

Rabbits were first imported into Australia with the First Fleet, but the plague of the animals started from a group of rabbits freed in Geelong, Victoria in 1859. By 1950 they had multiplied to 100,000,000,000!

The first lawyer in Australia was an ex-convict, and so were the first teacher and the first architect.

The world's most famous opal, The Queen of the Earth, was found at Lightning Ridge by one Jack Dunstan, who sold it for $200. John F. Rockefeller was later to pay a staggering $1,500,000 for it!

An unusual competition was held in 1961 between the towns of Stroud in Australia, Canada and England, when they met to contest which team could hurl bricks and rolling pins the furthest.

In cricket The Ashes commemorates the first victory by the Australian team against England, in England in 1882. There was a mock obituary for English cricket published in the *Sporting Times* after the 7-run victory. The ashes themselves are a cricket stump which was burned by some Melbourne women during the 1882-83 series, and presented to the Honourable Ivo Bligh, the English captain. Ever since, all test matches between the two countries have been for The Ashes.

The world's first milk bar was opened in Sydney in 1930 by Clarence and Norman Burt.

Australia's coastline is 12,210 miles long.

The coastline near Port Campbell

AUSTRALIAN GOLD

MEL GIBSON

'The sexiest man alive' is a hard tag to live with, but Mel Gibson does his best. Born in Peekshill, New York State, in 1956, Mel retains his American citizenship, but Australia is the place he calls home. His parents emigrated to Sydney when he was twelve.

Nicknamed 'Mad Mel' for his antics at school, he never wanted to be an actor. His sister applied for an audition for him at the National Institute of Dramatic Art in Sydney. He was accepted. He recalls, ''The first time I appeared on stage I couldn't remember the lines and I had the shakes!''

Fortunately he calmed down and made his first feature film, *Summer City*, while still at NIDA. When he graduated in 1977 he already had the star role of Mad Max to look forward to. And it was a success, hailed by critics as ''one of the finest achievements of Australian cinema''.

Despite his stardom, Mel Gibson remains a shy and private person. He lives quietly with his wife and children in a Sydney suburb close to the beach. They also enjoy spending time away from it all on their farm in Victoria.

The first Australian star to command $1 million a movie, he is among the top ten favourite movie stars in every country his films have been shown in. He is respected both within the business and by audience and critics alike. Like his hero, Humphrey Bogart, Mel Gibson is likely to be remembered not just as a sex symbol but as an actor of great worth.

HAYLEY LEWIS

Talented newcomers appear at every major international sporting event – but who could have guessed that a starring role in the 1990 Commonwealth Games would be so decisively played by an unknown schoolgirl from Brisbane?

Yet that is exactly what happened in the opening days of the games. 15-year-old swimmer, Hayley Lewis, unheralded by any publicity, quietly captured one gold medal after another. It soon became clear to the sporting world that she stood a chance of winning a record-breaking six gold medals.

In fact, Hayley only took the bronze in her final event, the 200m medley. Nevertheless her achievement is still extraordinary. Matching Canada's Graham Smith's 1978 record, she is only the second athlete ever to win six medals in a single games, and is the first woman swimmer ever to win five Commonwealth golds.

Not content with this, her performances in the 200m butterfly and 400m medley events, and as a team member of the 4 x 200m freestyle relay, all set new Commonwealth Games records. Hayley, a shy, retiring girl, has entered the world of international swimming a fully fledged star. ''I'm a real worry wart,'' she says. ''There were heaps of times when I didn't think I would make it to the trials.''

Young as she is, it seems certain that Hayley Lewis will be a name to look out for in the next Olympics.

SMOOTH TAKE-OFF

Which soap star started in *The Henderson Kids*, burned down Charlene's caravan in *Neighbours*, appeared in *Prisoner: Cell Block H*, starred in **Home and Away**, and has now taken to the skies in *The Flying Doctors*? Good looking Alex Papps, that's who, who now plays Nick Cardaci in the supersoap.

Alex, who starred as heart-throb Frank Morgan, is delighted at his most recent move. "I want to survive," he says. "I don't want to be a flash in the pan. I feel like *Flying Doctors* has been a step up – it's a step up from doing 2½ hours of video a week to two hours of film every two weeks."

Away from the rigours of work Alex says, "Sleeping is my favourite pastime!" Although now he has a little more time to himself he'll be more able to indulge his other hobbies of playing and listening to music at his home in Melbourne.

LUCKY LUCINI

It must be the first time that the son of a prime minister has appeared in a soap opera. Julian McMahon, who plays soldier Ben Lucini, is the son of former Australian PM, the late Sir William McMahon.

Julian won the part against tough opposition, and had to go through four auditions. Julian's previous claims to fame have been a TV ad for Levi jeans, and a role in another soapie, *The Power The Passion*.

"Life was hectic at the start but I've got much more of a grip on my character now and things are running smoothly," says Julian. "Ben is basically a great guy who comes from an Italian family and likes surfing and having a good time. But it's a case of love at first sight with Carly, and he decides to leave the army and stay in Summer Bay."

WERE HERE

EVERYBODY'S DAD

In real life he's the father of Jason Donovan. On screen Terry Donovan seems to be doing the rounds of the soaps as other people's dads.

First he popped up in Cooper's Crossing, playing the father of Nick Cardaci (played by Alex Papps) in *The Flying Doctors*. Jim Cardaci is a long distance lorry driver who causes a tragedy when he falls asleep at the wheel and runs into the back of a coach.

Now he's moved to Summer Bay, and appears in **Home and Away** as Brian Simpson, Bobby's mysterious missing 'father'. He causes problems for Fisher, with revelations about the teacher's secret past.

"I must have played about a dozen or more father roles," grins Terry. "I must be Australia's resident father." As for famous son Jason, Terry says he is looking for "the right project for myself and Jase. We do want to work together soon."

SOAP POPERA

Amanda Newman-Phillips, who did a spell in **Home and Away**, teamed up with fellow soap actor Greg Benson to try and break into the recording world when they visited London earlier this year.

Amanda hopes to follow in the footsteps of other soap stars like Kylie, Jason, Dannii and Craig McLachlan, who have successfully made the step from soaps into the pop world. Craig Thomson also had a crack at wooing the record bosses.

Lisa Laine, a Network 7 spokeswoman, said that both Greg and Craig had great singing voices, but it was Craig who attracted the most attention. CBS and EMI both expressed an interest. Greg and Amanda remained confident they too would land a contract, based on their demo song, which has Amanda singing the lead.

When Greg Benson was a young lad living out in the back of beyond his ambitions were aimed towards becoming a policeman or a lawyer, since modelling and acting were not things a country boy did. Not so many years later Greg was stripping down to his underpants several times a night on TV. It may only have been an advert but it certainly got him noticed!

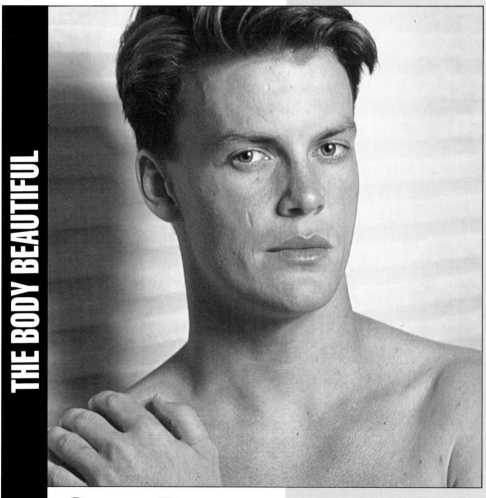

THE BODY BEAUTIFUL

Greg Benson

Matt

Sex appeal is something good looking Greg, who plays Matt Wilson in **Home and Away**, has in abundance. And it was what the ad-men spotted when it came to selling Levis to the Aussies, and doing a re-make of the successful Nick Kamen commercial. "It finally came down to two of us at the audition," recalls Greg. "I really wanted the job but I thought the other guy would get it. He had a better body." The

producers disagreed, and the success of the ad led to his being cast as Matt Wilson.

The role is a perfect fit for outdoor guy Greg. "Like all kids born near the ocean I spent most of my time on the beach. So it's no big deal that I can swim, scuba dive and windsurf." Greg still spends a lot of his spare time messing about in water. With his own boat moored on a lake he often escapes for the weekend to

34

waterski.

"My father's a policeman," says Greg, "so my older brother and sister and me did a lot of moving around when we were growing up. Now my dad and my dog, a bull terrier called Gus, live five minutes from the beach. Dad's still the most influential person in my life. We're great mates and spend a lot of time together."

The dog gets a look-in too. "Gus is my best mate. When I go surfing he's there with me and he comes out in the boat when we go fishing. When he was a puppy he used to sit on the windsurfing board with me, but now he's got too big!"

While the sporting side of Matt sits easily with Greg, he has experienced difficulty over girlfriends. Not that there would be any shortage of volunteers, but Greg has been particularly sensitive about not upsetting fans of the hunky lifeguard.

"I can swim, scuba dive and windsurf"

Amanda Newman-Phillips, who played Narelle, was on hand to help with a bit of subtle subterfuge. While she played the part of Greg's girlfriend in public, behind the scenes Greg was romancing Justine Clarke, bad girl Roo from the popular soap. Close friends of Justine said that as a result of adverse public reaction to her

may be an actress but I am a terrible liar. There have been so many times when I have had to stop myself holding his hand in public and giving him a kiss."

The next thing you know, another friend is describing Greg and Justine getting friendly at the launch of the new soap, *Family and Friends*. "Justine and Greg were totally engrossed in each other," said the friend. "They spent the entire

'I dream of finding a girl to share my life with"

character, Justine "thought it would get worse if fans knew she was with Greg. So she talked Amanda into claiming she was dating Greg to take the heat off her."

Meanwhile, on a promotional tour of Britain with Greg, Amanda was telling another story. "We have been trying to hide our affair so as not to break the hearts of all Greg's fans. I

evening canoodling. They hardly spoke to anyone else because they were having a good time and obviously didn't care who knew about it."

What the exact truth is is impossible to guess, for the following week Greg was saying, "I dream of finding a girl to share my life with but romances have never worked out." Confused? That's probably the whole idea. If you create enough phantom romances no one will ever guess which is real and which isn't. A beautiful body like that needs protection!

ON THE BEACH

On horseback at Port Douglas

Australia has 37,000 kilometres of coastline and all the major cities are next to the sea. Hardly surprisingly the Australians love their beaches.

After a hard day's work how about dropping down to the beach for a swim or a spot of surfing? For many Australians this is taken for granted. Sunshine, palm trees, soft white sands, a cool drink by your side . . . with nothing to do but lie back and soak it all up, the beach is the perfect place to relax. But if activity is what you like there are plenty of sports facilities from sailing to tennis and golf.

Naturally, being close to the ocean waves, many of the beach resorts feature a mouth-watering array of seafood, if you prefer to take your pleasures gastronomically. All this and sunshine too. In a country where almost everyone lives beside the sea the Australians grow up with the sea as part of their lifestyle.

Photos by courtesy of the Australian Tourist Commission

The Gold Coast, Queensland

RETURN TO NATURE

Thousands of people go swimming every day. It took a man called W.H.Gocher to make that possible, however. In 1902 bathing was banned between the hours of 6am and 8pm. Gocher, a newspaper editor, publicly announced that he intended to swim every day at nearby Manly Beach in Sydney.

Australian swimmers haven't looked back since, although some early opponents found it all positively indecent. 'The return to nature is too pronounced all together', they complained . . . but to no avail. The Aussies had fallen in love with the beach.

All Australia's beaches are publicly owned, so that you can swim anywhere. Some states even have nudist beaches if you want to tan from top to bottom!

A NATIONAL INSTITUTION

The variety of beaches is enormous. The distance around Australia is the equivalent of going from London to Sydney and back. There are the vibrantly busy urban beaches like Bondi, hundreds of miles of surfing beaches, or quiet, secluded bays with only the sea and the sky for company.

The water goes from crystal clear to turquoise and deep ocean blue. The sands may be a dazzling white, golden, or even blue, pink or black. From gentle lapping waters to rolling waves, each beach has its own character.

The Aussies feel at home on the beach. Whether beneath the starry skies of the Southern Cross, or the distant blue of sunlit days, the beach is a national institution.

Room to move: Broome in Western Australia

She was dubbed a teenage Joan Collins. She's been spat at and had names called at her in the street. But now she's a bright and happy nurse who has fallen in love, and she's liked by millions of people. A change of character has worked wonders for Justine Clark.

THE LITTLE RAGER CALMS DOWN!

Justine Clark

Roo

Only in the topsy-turvy world of Australian soaps could someone be elevated from superbitch to heroine in a few short months. For the rising star who found fame as bitchy Ruth Stewart in **Home and Away** is now winning hearts in rival soap, *Family and Friends*. And the talented actress thinks it's all wonderful.

Although only 19 years old, Justine is no newcomer to showbusiness. She landed her first

job at the tender age of seven working in commercials. The daughter of an actress and a singer, at twelve she won a part in *Mad Max II*, and later roles in *A Country Practice* and *GP*. But the pretty blonde hit the big time when she was offered the part of Roo when she was sixteen.

"Parents were very wary about letting their children even watch **Home and Away**," recalls Justine, "and frequently complaining of how we tackled topics like drugs, drinking and sex head on. But it was important that we did, because we might have helped some teenager out there who was dealing with the same pressures."

The scheming Roo certainly cut a swathe through Summer Bay. Poor Frank Morgan hardly knew what had hit him, and Roo's startling wedding day revelations were matched only by her determination to get him back – at the expense of his new love. Hardly an episode went by without her getting up to all sorts of tricks, manipulating boys and upsetting family and friends.

"Roo was a total bitch, horrible"

"She was a total bitch, horrible," says Justine. Aussie viewers nicknamed her 'the little rager'. And she was soon being recognized in the street. But it wasn't the sort of recognition which every actress would relish.

"The worst time," she remembers, "was in a shopping centre in Sydney's western suburbs. A few of us were making special appearances. Everyone else was cheered and I was booed. Then things got out of hand, and the fans began to charge us. Some were getting crushed and we had to bolt for it. And then I saw this one girl, I caught her eye and she spat at me, screaming 'You slut, you bitch!'"

"I never had any time to myself"

This sort of scene genuinely frightened Justine although she was used to the kind of letters fans sent in to the show's producers, saying: "Roo is a total cow and wrecks the whole show. She is always cheeky and gets away with

it. This influences other kids to think they can be like this. She should be fired."

But Justine beat them to it. After 18 successful months she decided to quit the show. "It may be a terrible mistake," she said at the time, "but it's now or never. When I first signed up I made the decision to only stay for 18 months. I never knew then that the show was going to be such a big hit. There was a lot of pressure on me to stay when my contract came up for renewal. But I was determined to stick to my guns and leave."

Justine also admits she needed a new and brighter challenge for her talents. "Sometimes you don't realize it, but when you're playing a character that's emotionally heavy it kind of interacts with your own life, and then you wonder why you're depressed. It's because you've been playing with your emotions all day. I needed to move on."

Leaving was easy, but moving on proved more difficult. Out of work she found life rather hard going. "I thought when I'd finished **Home and Away** I'd never work again. I just managed to put on a brave face and say I'm sure it's all for the best," says Justine. "I went through a bit of a trauma for a while."

It was, apart from anything else, an overnight change in lifestyle. "I missed the good old days when I was working in the studios," Justine says. "I was up at the crack of dawn. They worked us hard, but it was great fun. I never had any time to myself to develop hobbies so when it all stopped, I didn't know what to do."

After being offered three of four parts, which did her confidence no harm, Justine found herself in line for a part in a new soap, *Family and Friends* on Channel Nine. It was a complete change of character as nurse Carol Brooks. "She's bright and happy," says Justine. "A sweet girl with a good heart. She's a bit of a klutz with lots of energy."

Justine confesses she did have second thoughts about tying herself down with another ongoing role. "I did um and ah for a while," she says. "But I knew I was working with the same team who developed **Home and Away**, so I was confident and it was easier for me to make the decision." And the chance to explore a less intense character appealed. "This will be more of a good time. A lighter role and more fun."

Rejoining the hurly-burly of TV soaps, especially at the start of a new show, was to her liking as well. "It's wonderful. There's so much enthusiasm when you are all starting together."

Two other bright events came out of her departure from **Home and Away**. The first was that her real life flatmate, Mouche Phillips, stepped into her shoes in the soap. "It was so easy for Mouche," laughs Justine. "She went along and got the part – just like that." Justine and Mouche share a flat in Double Bay, one of Sydney's ritziest harbourside suburbs.

More important was the opportunity to come clean about her love life. She announced that she had fallen in love with fellow soap star Greg Benson. They had been secretly dating for months, but only let the cat out of the bag when she had safely left the series.

Said a close friend, "As she was getting so much abuse from playing the character of Ruth she feared it would get worse if the fans knew she was with Greg." Life should be a little easier now with easy-going Carol as her alter ego.

At nineteen Justine has a long way to go yet, but her heart is firmly set on one burning ambition. "You know my dream?" she asks, and you just know she's going to tell you. "One day, not now of course, but one day in the future when I'm ready – I'd love to see my name up in lights in the middle of London's West End."

Justine isn't counting her chickens yet, however. "You can be flavour of the month one day and nobody the next," she reflects wisely. It's hard to imagine talented Justine disappearing overnight.

EXIT ROGER

Roger Oakley
played super
beginning of **H**
Tom was dead
attack in Nove
gruelling sche
and it was tim

Roger, a N
the end of th
he'd tried
installing TV
worked as a
USA. His rol
established

He enjo
something
favourites
Rabbit, an
emergence

Roger li
they share
Roger mu
confessed
club scer
restaurant
Italian foo

He's er
regrets at
more TV
offers.

AUSTRALIAN GOLD

JACK BRABHAM

''If you stick with it and fight with it, it will often come right for you,'' says champion racing driver Jack Brabham in his autobiography. It was such positive thinking and determination that shaped Jack's amazing career.

Jack was born in 1926. His grandfather had emigrated in 1885, and his father had established himself as a greengrocer in a Sydney suburb. He encouraged his son's early love of cars.

During the war Jack served as an engineer in the Royal Australian Air Force. But it was when he was demobbed that Jack took up what was to become his life's work. He began by racing midget cars, becoming Australian champion for five years running.

In 1955 he scored his first big success, winning the Australian Grand Prix. Spurred on by encouraging results both at home and on the European circuit, Jack took the plunge and moved to England in 1957. In both 1959 and 1960 he won the World Championship in a Cooper-Climax, but left the Cooper team at the end of the following season.

Now Brabham the engineer came to the fore. He decided he was going to build racing cars, and set out to create the world-beating Brabham team, attracting drivers of the calibre of Piquet and Lauda.

Jack himself won Brands Hatch three times, the World Championship, and the Constructor's Cup for the Brabham-Renco car in 1966. He was the first man to win the titles in a car made by himself.

He was awarded the OBE for his services to motor racing, and retired in 1970 with 123 Formula One Grand Prix starts and 14 wins, including the French, Dutch, British, and German Grand Prix.

SHANE GOULD

She was called the 'Golden Girl' of the 1972 Olympics. 15 years old, with good manners and lovely golden hair, the Sydney girl won many hearts around the world.

Swimming eleven races in eight days she also won medals. Three Golds. And every one a world record. In fact she set eleven world records between 30 April 1971 and 11 February 1973.

Shane, called after her Welsh grandmother Shane Fish(!), applied herself with great dedication to swimming. It stood her in good stead during the hectic '72 Olympics. She opened with a victory in the 200m medley, followed very shortly by an easy win in the 400m freestyle, and a third gold in the 200m freestyle.

Freestyle was what she liked best – between December 1971 and August 1972 she held the world record for *all five* freestyle distances: 100m, 200m, 400m, 800m and 1500m. In the long distance she was the first woman to break the 17-minute barrier, swimming 16 minutes 56.9 seconds in Adelaide.

Both she and her parents worried about her growing up with so little chance to relax. Early mornings, constant training, strict dieting . . . her routine made her miserable. She went to California to recuperate, but she retired from competitive swimming, aged only 16 years and 9 months.

The golden girl who had thrilled the world with her remarkable swimming had glowed, memorably, for a mere 2½ years.

BLIND FREDDIE COULD SEE IT!

Australians speak English, or at least that's the language they took with them in the 18th and 19th centuries. But like languages everywhere, Australian English has developed in its own way, and created both its own new words and colourful sayings.

So, if you still reckon you speak the same language as the Aussies, read the following paragraph . . .

Blind Freddie could see that Mrs A is a stickybeak and a wowser. That might be fair dinkum, but asking her to mind her own business would be like sending a dill to find the bunyip. She may have kangaroos in the top paddock, but she's no drongo – she's ripper when it comes to organizing things and people. Even if she is as flash as a rat with a gold tooth sometimes, she does occasionally come a gutser. But few people would expect to come the raw prawn with her and not expect her to do her block.

Check it out with our Aussie dictionary to see if you translated correctly:

arvo	afternoon
beaut	fantastic, very good
bludger	a sponger
Blind Freddie could see it	something plainly obvious
Buckley's chance	one in a million chance
bunyip	Aussie version of the Loch Ness monster
come a gutser	make a mistake
crook	broken, no good, not well
dill	complete idiot
don't come the raw prawn	don't try and fool me
down the gurgler	wasted
do your block	lose your temper
drongo	person who's a waste of time
fair dinkum/dinkie die	the truth
flash as a rat with a gold tooth	showing off
garbo	dustman (garbage collector)
kangaroos in the top paddock	bats in the belfry, a bit crazy
larrikin	street tough
lurk	a shady scheme
neck oil	beer
new chum	someone newly arrived to live in Oz
ocker	country bumpkin, loudmouth
ripper	good
septic, seppo	American (septic tank: yank)
snags	sausages
stickybeak	busybody
tucker	food
uglier than a robber's dog	about as ugly as you can get!
walloper	policeman
wowser	killjoy
yakka	work

Without that word list most of us would be up a creek in a barbed wire canoe without a paddle – and that's dinkie die. G'day!

FLYING A
While Lanc
way round
has taken
ease. He
hooked. A
been bitte
Peter r
part shar
aircraft.
America
He ha
more th
want to
jumbo
loves b
supers
groun

AUSTRALIAN GOLD

CLIVE JAMES

The rotund, urbane host of *Saturday Night Clive* and many other television shows was born in Sydney in 1939. Following schooling in Australia, he completed his education at Cambridge where, as President of the Footlights society, he worked with Eric Idle and other members of what was to become the Monty Python team.

Finding that his talent was for wit rather than for comedy, Clive then teamed up with ex-Footlights singer Peter Atkin, producing satirical lyrics for a succession of critically acclaimed records.

In the late 1960s he also embarked on a more prominent career as a media commentator, breaking into television when he replaced Michael Parkinson as presenter of Granada TV's *Cinema*. In 1972 he became a regular columnist and television critic for *The Observer*.

During the 1980s Clive's TV appearances became more frequent, and he also achieved success as an author. His novels and essay collections, which take a typically wry look at society, have become bestsellers, as have the occasional volumes of autobiographical *Unreliable Memoirs*.

It seems likely that his dry humour and affable presence will display the sharper side of Australian humour in the British media for a long time to come.

SYDNEY NOLAN

Nolan, the landscape artist, was born a child of the Peace Comet. In 1916 this was visible in fine Australian autumn weather. His mother told him it had brought him, and he often recounted the story. The first of three children, he was born in Melbourne in April 1917.

In the 1940s a group of Melbourne artists, including Nolan, banded together as *The Angry Penguins*. Their work was very personal and impressionistic. They rejected all formal training, wanting to break with tradition.

They sought vitality in art, and spontaneous, creative art-making. And they wanted "the return to an authentic national vision", a truly Australian style of art. They used folklore and myth as their subjects.

As a child Sydney had visited the Glenrowan Aquarium in Melbourne where Ned Kelly's suit of black armour was on show, and Sydney's own grandfather had chased the famous outlaw. Sydney's series of Ned Kelly paintings is very childlike, with bright colours and strong images.

The series made Nolan the first famous painter of this Australian movement. His successful exhibitions in London, Paris and Rome opened the doors for others to gain international respect.

In 1949 he came to live in Cambridge, and in the 1950s and early 1960s was one of the best known painters at work in England.

WILD AUSTRALIA

The cuddly koala

Australia possesses one of the richest stores of wildlife in the world. Many of the plants and animals occur only on the Australian continent, having evolved to fit exactly into their particular environment. Others are as everyday to our own lives as the budgie, a native Australian bird. There's no doubt, however, that Australia has weird and wonderful wildlife. But as with any hot country, along with the beautiful and the spectacular there are also poisoners in paradise.

THE KOALA

Once almost hunted to extinction, these small furry marsupials are making a comeback, despite the bush fires that kill so many. The koala is one of the best known and most specialized of Australian animals.

It lives in forest and woodland, mostly in south eastern Australia, but fossil remains show that it was once found in the south west. It lives in trees, coming down only to cross to another. The leaves of the boab and jarrah trees form its main diet. It can digest only these and a few other species of eucalyptus.

The koala has a powerful grip and can climb even smooth trunks. After the young leave the pouch they are carried on the mother's back for several months. Few creatures look as cuddly as a koala.

The bearded dragon

The Tasmanian devil

Photos by courtesy of the Australian Tourist Commission

THE JARRAH TREE

There are around 500 varieties of eucalyptus in Australia. In some areas it is the dominant plant, and the ecological balance of the region depends on it.

The jarrah tree grows mostly in the south west. Between 25-35 metres high, the trees have flowers, woody ovoid fruits, and a fibrous bark. The oil and essential oils are used in medicine and flavourings.

It is the biggest contributor to the pulpwood and lumber trade, often being used to make pulp and chipboard for export. Environmentalists are disturbed by these huge clearances of timberland, which have a devastating effect on the wildlife which is dependent on the trees.

THE TAIPAN SNAKE

Rapidly becoming part of Australian folklore, the taipan snake is more venomous than a black mamba. Anything up to 4.5 metres long, it is one of the few poisonous snakes to lay eggs.

It was first discovered near Cooktown as late as the 1870s. The second specimen was not reported until 1922! There are now large numbers along the Gulf of Carpenteria to the north. They feed on rats and hunt mainly in the early morning or late afternoon.

A taipan bite is fatal to humans, and the known distribution is getting wider as more are being brought in for identification.

THE BUDGERIGAR

Native to Australia, the first budgerigar, or love bird, was discovered at Paramatta in 1804. They are not usually seen east of the Great Divide, except in periods of drought.

The first one shown in England was called an 'undulated parakeet', and they were later referred to as 'warbling grass parakeet' or 'the shell parrots'. The word budgerigar is probably Aboriginal in origin, meaning 'good bird' or 'good food'.

Nomadic grass-eaters, they sometimes gather in flocks so large that they darken the sky. In South Australia in April 1933 flocks passed overhead continuously for three hours.

Four aviary bred budgerigars were brought to England in 1840. In the wild they are always green, but they are now bred in various colours.

TASMANIAN DEVIL

As big as a medium sized dog, with black fur, a big pink mouth and huge white teeth, the Tasmanian devil looks fierce enough to have earned its name. This small version of a tiger is found only on the island of Tasmania.

Common in wooded areas, they feed on small animals like rabbits and wallabies. They are very strong, with powerful head, jaws and forequarters. They hunt at night, and will eat a whole wallaby apart from the skull.

Their appearance is frightening, but the young can be tamed. The mother carries three to four babies in a backward facing pouch. They are born in a nest deep in a hollow trunk or cave.

The duck-billed platypus

THE FUNNEL WEB SPIDER

This large, shiny black spider is highly poisonous and has caused several human deaths. The name comes from the design of its silk-lined nest. The entrance is funnel-shaped, and is usually under rocks or logs, or in a crevice in the ground.

It shelters here during the day, and then comes out at night to catch food on the ground, like beetles and other insects.

In summer mature males leave home in search of a mate. During the day it can hide in garages, sheds, even houses. It is most dangerous, however, to a human digging the garden. Disturbed, they rear up on their hind legs ready to strike.

THE DINGO

The dingo was probably the only animal imported into Australia by Aboriginal canoe. It was used as a hunting dog. One is quite capable of killing a full size kangaroo – and an adult male red kangaroo weighs 180lbs.

The oldest dingo remains are 7,000 years old. It would seem the tiger became extinct because of the coming of the dingos, who simply ate too much.

Many remain in the wild. These are like the 'yellow dog' of legend. Golden yellow fur with white markings on toes and tail tips is quite usual. A broad forehead and pricked ears make them look, as indeed they are, powerful and potentially dangerous.

Of course you don't have to go out into the wilds to see all of these creatures and plants. Many of them feature in wildlife parks, and in some parts of Australia the nearest place to see a funnel web spider could be your own bathroom!

Australian born Norman Coburn, who plays headmaster Donald Fisher in **Home and Away**, proudly declares he's a true Australian. But Norman's TV and stage apprenticeship was served both in Australia and in England, where he worked for many years before returning Down Under to success in the Aussie soap.

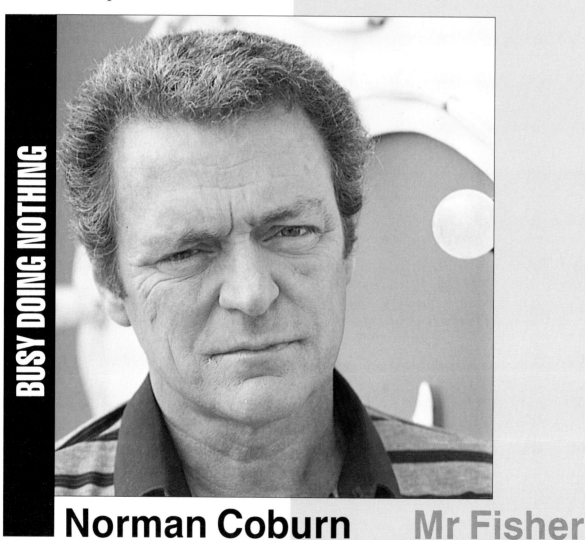

BUSY DOING NOTHING

Norman Coburn   Mr Fisher

"I was born in Paddington in Sydney," says Norman. "Then I was brought up in Earlwood in the suburbs. I really didn't have a regular teenage life at all. I started work at fourteen as an actor. It didn't worry me at all that I didn't do a lot of teenage things that young boys do."

Norman had caught the acting bug young, and was determined to succeed. His first breaks came in radio, and before long Norman was making a name for himself. "When I started in acting," he recalls, "it was on the radio. It was something I'd always wanted to do since I was very small. I guess it was the ham in me. Then I started playing all kinds of parts, from young kids to much older roles, and I found it all absolutely fascinating. It was a great time in the radio studios then, and we had a lot of fun."

Radio work led on to acting for the stage,

"England began to feel like home"

quite a different technique, but one which helped to broaden Norman's skills and experience as an actor. He worked with the Elizabethan Theatre Trust for a time, and in Sydney and did a couple of gruelling tours round Australia. "I think I've seen more of Australia than a good many Australians!" laughs Norman.

These tours were certainly not for the faint-hearted, but were the sort of experience that stand any young actor in good stead. Surviving the rigours of a long tour and still producing the goods on stage make *anything* that comes after seem easy by comparison. "Some of the places we had to play in were not up to the London Palladium standards," grins Norman, with a large measure of understatement, "but we always managed to get the show on."

For several years Norman toured the repertory circuit, playing exotic places like Farnham, Exeter and Western-Super-Mare. He also had parts in many of the popular TV series of the 1960s, including *Dixon of Dock Green*, *No Hiding Place* and *Compact*. "I stayed in England so many years," says Norman, "it almost began to feel like home." Indeed he married an English girl, and both his children, Nana and Troyt, were born here.

An amicable divorce came later, so amicable in fact that his ex-wife moved back to Australia with him, and they still see each other regularly. This isn't surprising when you realize that they both have flats in the same building!

The family have stuck together through the years. "I have my son, Troyt, living with me at the moment," says Norman. "But my daughter, Nana, shares a flat with a friend. We meet all the time though, as she's also in **Home and Away**. In fact Nan was considered for the series before I even auditioned for my schoolmaster role."

Norman is clearly happy with his daughter's success. "I was delighted when Nan showed an interest in acting – she started her career in commercials at the age of ten and has

"I didn't have a regular teenage life"

Norman, deciding that he'd seen enough of Australia for a while, thought it was time he set out to see the old country. A traditional route for many young Australian actors, Britain at once offers more theatres (and closer together!), more TV, more radio . . . in short, more work. "It was 1957 and I was only about nineteen or twenty at the time," recalls Norman, "so it was going to be a big adventure to me – something I was really looking forward to."

never looked back. Her role as bitchy schoolgirl Vicky is growing steadily more important," he adds with a father's pride.

While Norman is kept very busy with **Home and Away** he does have other interests. "I love the whole Australian scene," he says, "but somehow I get very little spare time to enjoy it. I've recently started to write film scripts. It would be wonderful if I could write blockbuster movies one day. That's one of my fantasies. But I guess my real hobby is doing nothing."

Merino sheep . . . let's see, 1-2-3-zzzzz

THE WORLD OF OZ

The first woman to fly was an Australian. Her name was Florence Taylor and she flew an early aircraft at Narrabeen, near Sydney in 1909.

Radio began in Australia in 1923, but television didn't get started until TCN Channel 9 opened in Sydney in 1956. They began broadcasting using the now standard 625 lines, while the UK (405 lines) and the USA (525) lagged behind technically.

Australia's largest spider is the *Selenvtypus plumipes*, a species of barking spider known to attack chickens and drag them into its burrow!

The kelpie, a smooth-haired, prick-eared sheepdog, was first developed in New South Wales around 1870, bred from Scottish collies. Kelpies can drive a chicken into a jam tin, so great are their working skills. This is known as tinning the chicken.

The first English ship to enter Australian waters was the *Tryal* in 1622. It sank on a reef. *The Lump* was the name given to the first boat built on the Australian mainland in 1879. It became the first ferry, the *Rose Hill Packet*, a 10-ton sloop.

New Zealand was once a dependency of New South Wales, but became a separate colony in 1841.

Australia is the least populated continent on the planet, with the exception of Antarctica.

Australia and Tasmania cover 2,967,909 square miles.

Brisbane was originally called Edenglassie; Melbourne was once known as Bearbrass; and Darwin used to be Palmerston.

The budgerigar, or love bird, is native to Australia. It was first exported to Britain around 1840.

Cobb & Company established a coaching firm in Melbourne in 1853. By 1870 they had 6,000 horses working every day. Their biggest coach was the *Leviathan*, which needed a team of 22 horses to pull it. Their last coach ran in 1924.

Tamworth in New South Wales was the first town to have electric street lighting in Australia, in 1888. Sydney had been the first with gas in 1841.

The world's longest bare knuckle fight happened in Daylesford, Victoria in 1855. Fought between James Kelly and Jonathan Smith, it lasted an epic 6¼ hours, and ended in a draw.

56

Photo courtesy of the Australian Tourist Commission

HOME + AWAY SEARCH-A-WORD

There's a whole heap of characters, actors and all sorts scrambled up in the Search-a-Word below. How many can you find? All the words are in straight lines, but they may read forwards, backwards, up, down – or even diagonally! Good luck with the search.

```
A S T A C E Y E N N A E L F R A
O R C R A I G M C L A C H L A N
A M E E E R A K A T E W O R C
F R A N K V E R R E E L A S E T
U I I D I I G T O O C I T S H R
A Y E E A D N I N E N A T I C A
I A S T E V E N A V A R A C T W
L B C A Y E N D Y S L A M E E E
S R Y O L Y F I I S S H X A L T
A E D L O L B B Q S I T E F F S
L M U A R N Y B R O Y R L H M G
O M J P H A R L O O T A C O A
H U T P U S C E R B O M B A T R
C S P I L L I H P N A M W E N O
I N K P O O L N O D R O G B H M
N U N O L A D N A M A S W I M T
```

Craig McLachlan ✓ Nicholas ✓   Steven ✓ Frank ✓   Bobby ✓ Stacey ✓ Nola ✓
The Bayside Diner ✓ Caravan ✓   Martha ✓ Floss ✓   Pippa ✓ Beach ✓   Ern ✓
Tom Fletcher ✓   Amanda ✓   Sydney ✓ Celia ✓   Carly ✓ Ailsa ✓   Roo ✓
Morag ✓   Gordon ✓   Leanne ✓ Lance ✓   Matt ✓   Sally ✓   Alf ✓
Newman Phillips ✓ Kate ✓   Swim ✓   Judy ✓   Adam ✓   Dive ✓   Alex ✓
Martin Dibble ✓   Summer Bay ✓ Greg ✓   Stewart ✓

57

HOME + AWAY

Vanessa Downing, the warm, caring foster mother Pippa Fletcher in **Home and Away**, desperately wants a baby of her own . . . just like the character she plays.

MOTHER INSTINCT

Vanessa Downing   Pippa

33-year-old Vanessa found it heart rending to play the scene where Pippa, who had given up hope of having a baby, found she was pregnant. Vanessa and her husband, Rodney, a theatre director, have wanted a baby for some time but unlike her screen character, she has not been successful.

"I'd do anything to have a baby of my own," says Vanessa. "I've tried for years but I don't think it's possible. If I was going to get pregnant it would have happened by now."

It was the part of Pippa that awoke the mother instinct in Vanessa. Until then she thought she detested babies. "I really had a thing about babies. I loathed them – not small children, just babies. If someone asked me to hold their baby I'd think 'Ugh, now what do I do?'"

58

Vanessa had always put her career first, and babies simply didn't fit into the plan. "I've always wanted to be an actress for as long as I can remember," Vanessa says. "I started going to drama classes when I was about 14. I later became one of those women who are interested in their career and didn't want children. I regret it now. I wish I'd had the sense to have children when I was younger."

In the absence of children, however, Vanessa's career did flower. She has worked extensively on stage, with both the South Australian Theatre Company and the Sydney Theatre Company. She has several film credits to her name, and has sung professionally as well as acted. **Home and Away** snatched her up when she was appearing at Sydney Opera House, and although she wasn't the original choice for the part Vanessa has made Pippa her own.

much I wanted a child of my own."

But it is other people's children that loom largest in Vanessa's life these days. Letters are constantly pouring in, a great many from British girls. "One girl couldn't talk to her parents," says Vanessa. "She felt I was the only mother she had. Another wrote saying her mother had fostered a child and this girl had taken her place in her mother's affections, so she was leaving home. She said, 'I wish my mother was like you.'"

It is perhaps not surprising that Pippa attracts so much affection from the fans. As Vanessa says, "She is good-hearted, honest and straight speaking." But reading such true stories of heartache has its effect on Vanessa. "It makes me feel very inadequate," she admits, but agrees that she has learnt a great deal about children's problems through her fan mail.

"I'd do anything to have a baby of my own"

Being a mother on screen was something new for Vanessa to tackle. "I thought I might have a problem when I had to handle baby Christopher," she recalls. "Once I started to handle a baby, though, there was a little bonding, only in a very small way, but it's there. Dylan, who plays Christopher, is gorgeous."

Dylan, it seems, made an almost instant conquest. "I fell in love with the baby when I held it in my arms in front of the cameras," confesses Vanessa. "It made me realize how

"I've always wanted to be an actress"

Meanwhile Vanessa will still keep trying for a child of her own, and says, "If the worst comes to the worst, perhaps I'll end up as a foster mum in real life." Trust that mother instinct – one way or another Vanessa is destined to become a real mum one of these days.

AUSTRALIAN GOLD

ROD LAVER

Red-headed Rod Laver is probably the most outstanding tennis player of all time. Of his generation he was probably also the wealthiest.

He won Wimbledon for two consecutive years, in 1961 and 1962. Indeed in 1962 he won six championships altogether, breaking all records, including achieving the Grand Slam of British, American and French titles.

He then left amateur tennis, but his standards did not fall. When the game became open to professionals (as it is now) for the first time in 1968, he returned triumphantly to Wimbledon to take the title once more.

In 1969 he won all four Open Championships - Australia, France, England and the USA, as well as the South African, Italian and German Gold Cups. His prize money in 1970 was more than $200,000, and in 1971 he became the first tennis player to earn over $1 million.

Small and quiet, he moved with great speed, and was given the nickname 'Rocket'. He had a powerful service, and with his English forehand grip he led the way for left-handers. His wrist and forearm were incredibly strong, the result of exercising by continually squeezing a squash ball between his fingers.

Rod Laver did a great deal to open tennis to professionals, helping to set up the Opens in Australia and New Zealand. His talent on the court will long be remembered by all those who saw him.

JOHN NEWCOMBE

Born in 1954, John Newcombe became an immensely successful international tennis star in the great Australian tradition. His dedication and talent were clear even in his youth. He won the New South Wales Schoolboy Championships at every age level. The Australian Junior Singles Championship was his for three years running in 1961–63.

Physically large and powerful, he played in the American style known as the 'Big Game'. This meant getting behind the ball and hitting it with a strong, firm-wristed action straight ahead. It is said that even when serving he used little wrist snap compared to other big servers. He developed great speed and good timing. This, with his ideal height and weight distribution, made him seem invincible.

In 1967 he won two major championships, Wimbledon and Forest Hills in the USA. He had arrived internationally. His fine, rugged game survived the opening of tennis to professionals, and although he lost to fellow Australian, Rod Laver, in 1968, Newcombe returned to take the Wimbledon singles title in both 1970 and 1971.

Handsome, strong, composed, he always looked dependable, both on and off the court. With Laver he ensured that the late 60s and early 70s were the golden age of Australian tennis.

HOME ➕ AWAY TOP 20

1. When did **Home and Away** first hit UK screens?
2. When was **Home and Away** first screened Down Under?
3. Who was Tom and Pippa's first foster child?
4. What were the first words spoken in **Home and Away**?
5. Who plays Ailsa Stewart?
6. In which city is **Home and Away** made?
7. Who devised **Home and Away**?
8. Who has played father to both Alex and Nicolle in different soaps?
9. What is the name of the cafe in Summer Bay?
10. What character does Peter Vroom play?
11. Who was accused of sending poison pen letters?
12. Which TV company shows **Home and Away** Down Under?
13. Who did Roo originally claim to be her baby's father?
14. Where did Neville and Floss once work?
15. What was Carly addicted to?
16. To whom did Martin 'accidentally' become engaged?
17. What company does Nicholas Walsh work for?
18. Who wrote the music for **Home and Away**?
19. Who are Bobby's real parents?
20. How many seagulls featured in the original opening credits?

HOME AND AWAY SEARCH-A-WORD

Photo by courtesy of the Australian Tourist Commission